HAPPENINGS IN NIGERIA

FLOODING IN NIGERIA AND HOW MANY ARE BEING RENDERED HOMELESS

EDWIN C.

TABLE OF CONTENT

- **Inferences regarding the cause of the flooding in Nigeria**

INTRODUCTION

As local authorities scramble to save hundreds of thousands of people being evacuated from their waterlogged homes, the death toll from this year's floods in Nigeria has grown to 603. According to the humanitarian affairs ministry, more than 1.3 million people have been homeless due to the crisis, which has touched 33 of Nigeria's 36 states.

There are now more concerns about disruptions to the food supply because at least 3,400 sq km (1,300 sq miles) of land have been flooded. Nigeria's northwest and central areas, which provide the bulk of the nation's food, are already endangered by conflict. This year's floods are the worst in more than ten years, especially in its coastal regions. According to the authorities, the calamity was caused by unexpected rains and the discharge of extra water from the nearby Lagdo Dam in Cameroon.

In Yenagoa, the capital of Bayelsa state in southern Nigeria, Al Jazeera's Ahmed Idris said that residents are rushing to the city to receive assistance from the authorities. According to Idris, the bad news is that rain is anticipated to continue falling for the upcoming days after pouring down for the previous three days. He stated, "The water levels are rising to a worrying level. "The force of the water's flow has likewise grown more ferocious. Continued flooding from upstream is coming this way. According to the Internal Displacement Monitoring Center, the flooding has worsened a humanitarian catastrophe in Nigeria, where violence has forced more than three million people from their homes, particularly in the turbulent northern region.

Climate Crisis

Six hundred people have died in Nigeria's floods, and many more have fled.

According to authorities, at least 603 people have died in this year's floods, and more than 1.3 million have been displaced.

Nigeria flood

Annual flooding occurs in Nigeria, especially along the coast, but this year's flooding is the worst in more than ten years [File: George Esiri/Reuters].

As local authorities scramble to save hundreds of thousands of people being evacuated from their waterlogged homes, the death toll from this year's floods in Nigeria has grown to 603.

According to the humanitarian affairs ministry, more than 1.3 million people have been homeless due to the crisis, which has touched 33 of Nigeria's 36 states.

There are now more concerns about disruptions to the food supply because at least 3,400 sq km (1,300 sq miles) of land have been flooded. Nigeria's northwest and central areas, which provide the bulk of the nation's food, are already endangered by conflict.

A statement from the office of President Muhammadu Buhari said that he had ordered: "everyone concerned to work for the restoration of normalcy."

Nigeria's floods are the worst in more than ten years, especially in the coastal regions, where flooding occurs yearly. According to the authorities, the calamity was caused by unexpected rains and the discharge of extra water from the nearby Lagdo Dam in Cameroon.

In Yenagoa, the capital of Bayelsa state in southern Nigeria, Al Jazeera's Ahmed Idris said that residents are rushing to the city to receive assistance from the authorities.

According to Idris, the bad news is that rain is anticipated to continue falling for the upcoming days after pouring down for the previous three days. He stated, "The water levels are rising to a worrying level. "The force of the water's flow has likewise grown more ferocious. Continued flooding from upstream is coming this way. He stated, "The water levels are rising to a worrying level. "The force of the water's flow has likewise grown more ferocious. Continued flooding from upstream is coming this way.

According to the Internal Displacement Monitoring Center, the flooding in Nigeria has exacerbated a humanitarian catastrophe where more than three million people have been displaced by conflict, particularly in the turbulent northern area.

Five states are still at risk of flooding through the end of November, according to the Minister of humanitarian affairs, Sadiya Umar Farouq.

Farouq stated, "We are urging the respective state governments, local government councils, and communities to get ready for more flooding by moving those who live in flood plains to high grounds.

States affected by flooding in Nigeria.

The humanitarian affairs minister said Buhari provided the flood victims with 12,000 metric tonnes of foodstuff last week. Due to devastating floods that have left dozens of people dead or homeless and the failure of state governments to take preventive action, lives and property throughout the country, particularly in coastal regions, are in danger. Because of the severe floods, many people get chills when clouds gather because they signify disaster.

Despite warnings, citizens' and officials' lack of preparation has worsened the situation.

Already, 18 states have been severely impacted by the yearly recurrence.

These states are Plateau, Kano, Kaduna, Niger, Benue, Adamawa, Jigawa, Taraba, Bauchi, Anambra, Ebonyi, Yobe, Edo, Delta, Kogi, Lagos, Ogun, and Ekiti.

There have been fewer than 300 fatalities in the United States in the past year, so there are worries that the severe rains expected in September, October, and November may cause much more suffering and loss of life.

DAM carnal

Worldwide organizations like SCI (Save the Children International). According to Sunday Vanguard's findings, there haven't been any tangible steps taken to move people living in low-lying areas or address other urban issues identified as the cause of recurring flooding, except for some public awareness campaigns.

Several states have significantly fallen short in preventing preventable damaging floods.

In reality, Sunday Vanguard noted that they had neglected to build structures like dams, canals, storm drains, and other infrastructure to divert floodwaters away from areas where they knew a significant likelihood of a disaster occurring.

NEMA, the Ministry of Water Resources, the National Emergency Management Agency, and even some other organizations have warned about this. According to the SCL, flooding in Nigeria and the Niger Republic has already claimed the lives of more than 75,000 children.

According to the Presidency, 277 people were hurt nationwide, and more than 500 000 were affected by severe flooding in August.

However, in a statement, the Presidency reiterated the gravity of this year's negative rainfall pattern and the threats that Nigerians face.

Torrential

In August, NEMA warned that 32 states and 233 LGAs were at risk of flooding in the upcoming months.

During a national consultative workshop on 2022 flood preparedness, mitigation, and response in Abuja, the agency's director-general, Mr Mustapha Ahmed, stated that each state has received warning letters and maps indicating the common areas to experience flooding.

Following the NIHSA's Annual Flood Outlook, Ahmed added, "We have also created risk maps for susceptible local government regions."

Additionally, he asserted that regional and municipal emergency management committees must take the initiative.

He said that more than 100 towns were affected by the daily average of over 50 flood catastrophe alerts sent to NEMA.

According to the NEMA DG, improvements would have occurred if states had taken the reports submitted to them seriously.

Ahmed speculated that "maybe they're not taking the reports we're sending them very seriously."

"As soon as it publishes a report, we provide the risk mapping to states, outlining the disaster risk zones. So, these states own all this data.

We believe states should create mitigation strategies in light of all this information.

Suleiman Adamu, the Minister of water resources, had already warned that the flood prediction for September, October, and November was cause for alarm.

According to Adamu, 233 local government areas in 32 states and the FCT are probably in flood-risk zones. In comparison, 212 local government areas in 35 states, including the FCT, are located in moderately probable flood-risk areas

IMPACTED STATES

The remaining 392 local government areas are located in locations with a high likelihood of flooding.

The following states have a very high likelihood of experiencing flooding: Adamawa, Abia, Akwa Ibom, Anambra, Bauchi, Bayelsa, Benue, Cross River, Delta, and Ebonyi.

Others include Ekiti, Edo, Gombe, Imo, Jigawa, Kaduna, Kano, Kebbi, Kwara, Lagos, Nasarawa, Ogun, Ondo, Osun, Oyo, Rivers, Sokoto, Taraba, Yobe, Zamfara, and the Federal Capital Territory.

But according to the Minister, eight states—Rivers, Bayelsa, Cross River, Delta, Edo, Lagos, Ogun, and

Ondo—will contend with tidal surges and a rise in sea level in 2022.

He further predicted that flash floods and urban flooding would occur in several areas of several major cities, including Lagos, Kaduna, Suleja, Gombe, Yola, Markurdi, Abuja, Lafia, Asaba, Port Harcourt, Yenagoa, Ibadan, Abeokuta, Benin City, and Birnin Kebbi.

Additionally, there are Sokoto, Lokoja, Maiduguri, Kano, Oshogbo, Ado Ekiti, Abakaliki, Awka, Nsukka, Calabar, and Owerri.

Even though millions of dollars worth of property and lives had already been lost to devastating floods in specific places before the warning, knowledge has done nothing to lessen the effects of flooding.

Residents in the states, as mentioned earlier, are currently vulnerable to deadly floods.

PLATEAU: Destructiveness and deaths

In Plateau State, flooding decimated specific communities, leaving hundreds homeless and at least seven individuals reported dead.

At the Nyelleng and Gwabi settlements in the Pankshin Local Government Area, LGA, of Plateau State, the tremendous rain that fell from August 22 to 24, 2022, washed away four persons and injured others, including a pregnant mother.

Settlements in the area were inundated, and the single bridge connecting them to neighbouring communities was also drowned.

Mr and Mrs Daniel Goma, along with two other people, were among those washed away.

Residents trying to wade through the flood on their way home from a nearby local market lost their lives.

Likewise, two persons passed away, while others were hospitalized. Flooding at Rikkos, Gangare, and other communities in Jos North LGA destroyed property worth millions of Naira.

One person in Langtang South LGA passed away due to the flood, which destroyed crops.

There were no fatalities in Mikang LGA, but heavy rains demolished some homes, leaving the residents without a place to live, and washed crops away in certain areas, including Garkawa, Lalin, and Tunku.

The enormous floods caused by the rain that poured in Qur'an-Pan LGA between August 15 and August 28 caused devastation, drowned villages, and destroyed homes, roads, bridges, and other infrastructure.

Bridges and farmlands were washed away, affecting Ball, Kwa, Doemak, Kwalla, Kwande, Namu, and other communities.

The state administration has nonetheless mandated the urgent restoration of the two collapsed bridges, one connecting Doemak to Bwall and the other Doemak to Doemak.

KANO damaged 6,417 homes, marketplaces, and roadways.

The downpour recorded in Kano State caused flooding that inundated streets, homes, and markets, among other things.

Poor drainage and garbage management are two primary causes of floods in the state.

Every time it is about to rain, inhabitants continue to be terrified because of the recurrence.

SEMA, the emergency management agency for Kano State, revealed that floods and windstorms had destroyed 6,417 homes and other buildings worth N541.6 million since April.

Dr Saleh Jili, the executive secretary, claimed that 10 LGAs had reported the events. Doguwa, Kibiya, Kiru, Rano, Danbatta, Tsanyawa, Gwale, Ajingi, Dawakin Kudu, and Albasu were the impacted locations, according to Jili.

He stated that due to the state's flooding and windstorms, "nine people were murdered, 6,417 homes were destroyed, nine people were injured, and property worth N541.6 million was lost."

He added that to gather comprehensive data and help victims, the agency had sent personnel to all ten impacted areas to perform assessment exercises.

As a result of a shortage of drainages, the state's principal highways and roundabouts are progressively becoming impassable to motor vehicles.

Sharu Sagiru, the chairman of the textile market, also known as Kantin Kwari, claimed that flooding caused the market to lose more than N4.5 billion.

More than 800 stores with a variety of items were also impacted, according to Sagiru.

NIGERIA: Victims get payment to flee flood-prone locations

Flooding appears to be worse in Niger State.

Catastrophic in light of where four hydroelectricity dams are.

When the dams are filled, they occasionally open their gates, flooding buildings and destroying crops.

The condition was most damaged when 20 of the state's 25 LGAs were submerged due to extreme flooding two years ago.

According to credible reports, flooding in Niger has claimed some lives this year.

One of the fatalities occurred in Rafi, and the other two in Kontagora LGA.

In addition to the lives lost, numerous homes, farms, and ditches, among other things, have been destroyed.

Two deaths were reported in the region, while 237 people were affected by the flood, according to Alhaji Shehu Pawa, chairman of Kontagora LGA, who confirmed the event.

In addition to providing 500 bags of cereals, including rice, maize, and millet, Governor Abubakar Sani Bello also provided 100 textiles to the flood victims in Kontagora.

To prevent similar incidents in the future, Bello ordered the demolition of any structure built alongside rivers.

"Many people who were impacted were offered compensation to move out, but they declined. He said that we would proceed to demolish the homes along the waterways.

The necessary design for a long-term remedy to floods will be completed by the end of September, according to the state's commissioner for the environment, Daniel Habila Galadima.

BENUE: River dredging is required.

Every year, communities in Benue State experience floods that leave a path of destruction in their wake.

Communities in Makurdi, the state capital, have been devastated despite nearly all preventative measures to stop the yearly occurrence.

Residents have had to deal with flood waters well into every rainy season, whether they live in settlements along the River Benue's edge or those nearby, including those right in the middle of the state capital.

The calamity has not spared Wadata Rice Mill, Angwan Jukum, Achussa, Behind Police Zone 4, Ishaya Bakut Road, Idye, the Living Faith Church neighbourhood on Naka Road, Wurukum, or any other locations.

A similar occurrence occurred in Benue in 2012 when most of Makurdi and its surroundings submerged, displacing impacted families from their homes.

Then came the 2017 catastrophe, which saw homes, cars, farms, and more than 100,000 people left without a place to live due to torrential rains and the opening of a dam in neighbouring Cameroon.

No exception applies to this year. Massive flooding had already occurred in Makurdi, although it was not on the same scale as the disasters of 2017 or 2019, when areas of the city were submerged, displacing and destroying hundreds of families.

To protect the state from the recurring floods, Governor Samuel Ortom has urged the federal government to take action to dredge the River Benue.

The governor stated that dredging the River Benue remained the most excellent method to prevent flooding in Benue State while announcing one of his visits to some of the state's affected villages. The recurring issue of flooding in the state will be permanently solved if the river is dredged.

EDO Communities cut off

To lessen the effects of the impending flood in Edo State, NEMA warned communities of its imminence and asked them to remove drainages, especially in flood-prone regions.

Mr Dahiru Yusuf, Head of NEMA Edo Operations Office, placed the call in Benin.

According to Yusuf, the warning became necessary when the seasonal climate prediction for 2022 indicated that there would be heavy rainfall across the nation.

"Drainages, culverts, and all streams should be removed for free flow of water without hurting buildings and also to lessen the impact of flood, especially in the metropolitan centres," he stated.

Since regular rainfall would raise the water levels of several rivers throughout the state, the NEMA official recommended riverine populations begin migrating to higher lands when the volume of water increased.

According to Yusuf, the growing season in Edo State is expected to be longer than average in 2022.

According to the officials of the frontline local governments, this prediction is already coming true in Edo State, where a rise in water volume has cut off certain villages.

He claimed that villages along the river banks would experience flooding when water levels rose, which would destroy homes, buildings, and crops.

According to Yusuf, the expected rainfall in the LGAs of Etsako East, Etsako Central, and Esan South-East would be slightly above average and likely result in flooding along the banks of the River Niger.

In order to prevent the loss of lives, resources, and livelihoods, he urged farmers in the region to follow the forecasts.

OVER 50 DIED IN JIGAWA

In Jigawa State, rainstorms and windstorms have claimed the lives of no less than 50 people.

Thousands of homes were demolished, and people were relocated due to the development.

According to Yusuf Sani, Executive Secretary of Jigawa State Emergency Management Agency, the deaths have been noted since the start of the rainy season. Nearly all 27 LGAs, according to Sani, were impacted.

Approximately 50 people have died, he claims, as a result of a rainfall that essentially caused building collapses.

In addition to Kafin Hausa, the impacted LGAs include Malam Madori, Hadejia, Guri, Auyo, Birniwa, Jahun,

Miga, Kiyawa, Birnin Kudu, Kaugama, Babura, Gwaram, Dutse, and Kirikasamma LGAs.

The flood caused the displacement of hundreds of residents while destroying several homes, buildings, farms, livestock, and other properties.

Farmers whose farms were also looted make up the majority of the victims.

In Dutse's Karnaya village, some 2,051 people were displaced.

Ten fatalities in ADAMAWA in 15 hours of rain.

The death toll is also high in Adamawa State, where a single LGA alone recorded ten flood-related fatalities.

Dr Suleiman Muhammad, the executive secretary of the Adamawa State Emergency Management Agency, claims that the flood caused dozens to be displaced from their homes and killed ten people in several areas of the state's Girei LGA.

The incident specifically took place in and around Jabbi Lamba town.

After 15 hours of relentless rain across the state, the incident occurred, Sunday Vanguard learnt.

TARABA: Three days of precipitation.

Communities in Taraba State are currently a victim of flooding. Rains that have destroyed farmlands in the process have already overwhelmed some people.

For instance, the Ibi Local Government Area's riverine village of Damper saw terrible flooding that nearly engulfed the entire community.

Three days of three-day-long floods caused devastation by destroying residents' possessions and properties brought on by severe rain.

19 out of 20 Local Government Areas (LGAs) in BAUCHI are in ruins.

Only one of the 20 LGAs in Bauchi State escaped the devastation of the flood.

The flood caused many people to be displaced from their homes and farmlands in 19 LGAs around the state.

At least ten people have died, and numerous hectares of farmland and homes have been lost in several regions of the state.

The LGAs that have been most severely affected include Jama'are, Giade, Misau, Dambam, Zaki, Darazo, Kirfi, Itas-Gadau, Shira, Gamawa, and Toro. The state government claims that 12 of the 19 impacted areas are severely affected.

CITY OF LAGOS FLOODING IN NIGERIA

Lagos suffers from severe floods yearly, which cause devastation because it is a coastline state.

Lagos' urban flooding is caused by several factors, including its natural propensity for flooding as well as the failure of the authorities to stop preventable incidents.

Canals, drainage systems, and other waterways are either neglected or blocked by faulty construction in the city.

Furthermore, environmental cleanliness receives little attention from municipal governments.

Both the people and the administration fail to observe the weekly sanitation that is meant to take place.

Due to the state's Ministry of Environment and other relevant authorities' negligence, Nigerians struggle with the painful repercussions of the problem every year.

Urban floods, which frequently submerge homes and ruin property worth millions of dollars, have been a problem for locals this year.

Nine people were recently trapped in the Mende neighbourhood of Maryland in Lagos as a building began to sink. In the state's Alimosho LGA, two additional deaths have been verified.

Seven people, including three siblings and four adults, perished as a result of the flooding that was experienced in the state, according to Ibrahim Farinloye, coordinator of NEMA's Lagos State Territorial District.

For instance, the state was severely flooded, and some citizens have swept away to their deaths during three days of rain between July 8 and July 10.

Agege, Lekki, Ajah, Victoria Island, Ifako, Oworo, Ogudu, Ayobo, Gbagada, Iyana-Ipaja, and Ebutte Metta are among the worst impacted places.

Anambra flash flood

NEMA announced that Ginikanwa Izuoba died in the Enugu-Otu, Aguleri flood in Anambra State. According to Mr Thickman Tanimu, the agency's acting state coordinator in Anambra, Izuoba perished when the flood's effects caused her house to collapse.

Further information from Tanimu indicates that the flooding in Anambra State has so far resulted in the displacement of at least 651,053 people across six local government areas. With 286,000 casualties, Ogbaru has the most, according to NEMA's records for Anambra. Following 237,000 and 103,000 victims each, respectively, are the Anambra West and East Local Government Areas (LGAs). Ten thousand three hundred forty-five victims have been reported in Awka North LGA, compared to 9,240 flood cases and 5,468 displaced people in Ayamelum.

NEMA visited the LGAs of Anyamelum, Mkpunando, Umunteze, Igbedo, and Inoma Ifite-Ogwari in Anambra

East with representatives from the State Emergency Management Agency (SEMA).

A task force comprised of the Deputy Governor, Commissioners for Local Government, Health, Power, and Water Resources was established by Prof. Charles Chukwuma Soludo after he made an equal number of visits to all the affected areas. The task force's immediate goal is to engage the displaced people and see that they receive the necessities they require.

According to Tanimu of NEMA, the evaluation team noticed that the flood had flooded homes, farms, schools, hospitals, police stations, churches, and other crucial infrastructure. Because the access routes to the settlements were attacked, we conducted the evaluation visit from a boat.

Anambra SEMA received praise from Tanimu for "taking some preemptive measures to lessen the impact of the tragedy." Identifying 13 Internally Displaced People's (IDP) camps, hiring camp managers and support staff, and activating health workers to work with the camp residents were some of the actions conducted. The Ifite-Ogwari and Igbakwu Health Centers are the camps that have so far been made active.

The evaluation tour is the first action the federal government must take, in Tanimu's words. The agency's administration has been informed of our findings, and in light of those findings, they are now free to distribute humanitarian supplies as necessary. We urge the locals to relocate to the holding camps once more to prevent future casualties.

The situation in the country is urgent. Schools in the villages along the rivers have been closed. Clothing, diapers, beds, sanitary products, various food items, and other humanitarian supplies are urgently needed to stabilize a dire situation that the states cannot handle on their own.

Five-hour deluge in Ekiti

Ado-Ekiti is prone to flooding, which has persisted despite efforts by the state government and other pertinent organizations to stop it from wreaking havoc on the state capital.

Residents of the Balemo and Tinuola sections of Afao Road were displaced in 2021 due to excessive rain that ruined commodities worth millions of Naira.

Residents of the Ado-Ekiti metropolis's suburbs along Federal Polytechnic Road, including Oshodi, Ilupeju Avenue, Ureje, Ita Eku, and Temidire Eminrin, suffered significant property losses due to flooding three days ago.

According to information received, a rainfall that started at 10 pm on Sunday and continued until roughly 3:22 am on Monday caused the flood.

Residents of the Temidire Emirin neighbourhood were hardest damaged as the Ureje River's rushing water grew and spilt the bank.

Jude Ajulo, a resident of Temidire Emirin, told Sunday Vanguard that at about 2 am, while they were resting, they awoke to find their homes underwater.

Another speaker, Taiwo Osaleye, a resident of Oshodi along Afao Road, urged the government to dredge the Elemi River, which runs through the area, to end the flood situation.

The Ekiti State Emergency Management Agency, or SEMA, stated that residential property and life safety were its top priorities.

"You all know that the administration of Ekiti State is serious about disaster management policy," SEMA's director Olajide Borode remarked. The current administration places high importance on property and human safety, and we won't play around with it. Our representatives are currently in the impacted areas to get accurate information to help the government decide how to respond to the tragedy.

Borode continued by saying that SEMA had selected three municipalities that would likely be impacted by the impending flooding and had advised residents of the communities downriver to move to safer regions.

OGUN: Fish farmers lose N500m in investment, and two people die.

In Ogun State, the flood that caused devastation in several areas of the nation claimed no less than two lives and destroyed property worth millions of Naira, including multiple fish farms.

Two adult males were killed while crossing a road in the Ifo local government region of the state during the severe rains of July 8 and 9.

Approximately 200 fish farmers in Ikangba/Agoro in the state's Odogbolu local government area calculated their losses on the same day that the flood struck their clusters of fish ponds, wiping out an investment they estimated to be worth over N500 million.

Over 200 impacted farmers are dispersed throughout five fish farm clusters in Ifeoluwa, Asejere, Progressive, Joye, and Kajola, according to Mr Lazarus Okole, Chairman of the Ikanga/Agoro Fish Farmers Association, who made this announcement.

Although the farmers had previously experienced flooding, he argued that the scale and impact of their losses could not be compared to the disaster in July. He also warned that many farmers might pass away from shock due to the failures unless the federal and state governments came to their aid.

Inferences regarding the cause of the flooding in Nigeria

According to Paul Nwosu, Nigeria and Cameroon should solve the Lagdo Dam's water release.

The annual tragedy of raging flooding in our nation is at its worst this year. The somewhat uncontrollable floods are thought to have claimed the lives of more than 300 people.

Twenty-seven of Nigeria's 36 states are currently experiencing flooding. The deluge pouring from Lokoja, the capital of Kogi State, threatens even Abuja. Many families have been impacted, and displaced people keep growing. Farmland covering thousands of hectares has been damaged. Given the severe disruption to the agricultural supply chain, hunger is a clear and present risk.

The State Emergency Management Agencies (SEMA) can barely handle the onslaught of water, and the National

Emergency Management Agency (NEMA) is at its wit's end. Nigeria is, in fact dealing with an extreme catastrophe. Manzo Ezekiel, the NEMA spokeswoman, emphasized that "this is the highest we have had since 2012."

Nigeria now experiences flooding each year, which has become a recurring issue. This is generally a result of environmental regulations not being followed, a lack of infrastructure for flood prevention, and a lax approach to dealing with the threat of flooding over time. It appears as though the government would never take preventative action to stop the flooding. Once the floods start, they are seldom caught off guard. The blame game never ends when it comes to "Water overflowing from several local rivers, unexpected rainfalls, and the release of surplus water from Lagdo Dam in neighbouring Cameroon's northern area" are blamed for the regular flood.

The water flow issue from the Lagdo Dam in Cameroon has already been brought up twice, and it needs to be addressed immediately at the highest level between Nigeria and Cameroon. It defies logic for Cameroon's leadership to appear as if they are uninformed of the destruction caused by overflowing waters from their dam in Nigeria. We must stop the heartbreaking economic defeat and pain. To stop Cameroon's blatant disrespect for Nigerian lives, property, and means of subsistence, the federal government must take action economically, politically, and internationally.

Locally, the Nigeria Hydrological Services Agency had forecast that this year would see more floods than the previous year due to "excessive rainfalls." NEMA has also warned states of "severe implications" in the following weeks and months. Additionally, two of the nation's dams have begun to overflow. Mustapha Habib Ahmed, a representative of NEMA, stated: "I want to advise all the governments of the frontline states to relocate towns at risk of flooding, find safe higher grounds for evacuating people, and appropriate preposition stockpiles of food and non-food supplies."

According to the currently available reports and Yusuf Sani Babura, the director of the Jigawa State Emergency Management Agency, more than 20 persons have died due to flooding in Jigawa State in the Northwest in the last week. In addition, Jigawa has seen 91 flood-related fatalities this year, more than any other state in the nation. We are dealing with severe floods that are out of our control, Babura lamented. Despite our best efforts, we were unable to stop it.

The same Lake Nyos endangered 300,000 lives on December 20, 2005. But to lower the amount of carbon dioxide in the water, a degassing device has now been erected at the lake. There were worries that Lake Nyos Dam would fail in September 2012, causing massive flooding that would destroy numerous Nigerian states.

It's unlikely that the terrible body of water Cameroon dropped on Nigerians may be checked by a bilateral panel of flooding from both nations, much like the lethal gas from Lake Nyos was restrained. To permanently resolve the issue of the over-watering Lagdo Dam, the two countries must work together.

Nigeria can no longer afford to play the role of the prominent African brother and keep dying quietly as her neighbour's property destroys her people and their means of subsistence during this trying time.

Anambra State Commissioner for Information

INTRODUCTION

www.ingramcontent.com/pod-product-compliance
Lightning Source LLC
LaVergne TN
LVHW020526160826
845677LV00015B/3929

* 9 7 9 8 3 5 9 3 1 6 7 0 5 *